BILLY SUNDAY

W. Terry Whalin

Illustrated by
Ken Save

PUBLISHING, INC.
Uhrichsville, Ohio

Published by Barbour Publishing, Inc.
        P.O. Box 719
        Uhrichsville, Ohio 44683
        http://www.barbourbooks.com

 Member of the
Evangelical Christian
Publishers Association

Printed in the United States of America.

Prologue

The New York City tabernacle was packed. Thousands of people squirmed in their seats waiting for the preacher to begin. With his distinguished sharp jaw and ram-rod straight posture, Billy Sunday marched toward the high pulpit.

The crowd clapped and cheered. Many of them waved white handkerchiefs as the choir sang the "Battle Hymn of the Republic." Sunday climbed the steps to the pulpit like a fighter entering the ring.

With a sweeping motion, Sunday began, "If you want to live in sin, all right, live in sin, and go to hell at the end." He moved across the stage and banged his fist on the pulpit. No one even thought about drifting to sleep. "Everything that the devil's in favor of, I'm against," he said. Skipping across the stage, Sunday shadowboxed the devil. He then slid like he was crossing home plate with the winning run. "The time has come to present yourself before the Lord. Acknowledge your wrong and see what God can do for you." Hundreds came forward that night to make a personal commitment to Christ.

The following pages will introduce you to the life of William Ashley Sunday. Sunday preached over 20,000 times during his life or an average of 75 times per month. More than 100 million people heard him proclaim the Good News about Jesus.

"Is he going to be OK, Doctor?"

1

A Rough Beginning

"Is he going to be OK, Doctor?" Only hours before on this cold winter day, November 19, 1862, Billy Sunday was born. The baby was small and Mary Jane (or Jennie) wondered if her son would live. Lying in bed, Jennie looked across at the beams of their little log cabin in Ames, Iowa. The rough floor boards creaked as they walked on the wood to cook over a stone fireplace. Sometimes the wind swept through the bark logs of the cabin, which were plastered with clay. Their little cabin looked pretty much like their neighbors' in this Midwestern pioneer area.

Only four months before Billy's birth, his father William Sunday marched off to join the Union army.

One day, he wrote home, "If my child is a boy, I'd like to call him William Ashley." That letter was one of the last times the family heard from William Sunday.

While he crossed a stream with the army, Mr. Sunday caught a cold and became ill. Because of the lack of medicine and good doctors, many people didn't recover from these illnesses. Mr. Sunday died within a few days.

Sadness hung in the air at Billy's birth. His two older brothers, Edward, aged two, and Albert, aged four, made Billy's birth even a greater challenge to his mother. Jennie's father, Martin Corey lived near the Sunday home. One of the first settlers in the area from Ohio, Martin Corey was known as "Squire." Grandfather wore a coonskin cap, rawhide boots and blue jeans. A colorful character, Grandfather drank his coffee from a saucer instead

Jennie's father, was known as "Squire."

of a cup and ate his peas with a knife. He was well-known and respected throughout this section of the country.

Jennie Sunday struggled to survive and care for her three boys. Before Billy was two years old, his mother remarried Leroy Heizer. He became the official guardian for Jennie's three sons.

During his first three years of life, Billy was almost constantly sick. Finally an old French doctor who traveled throughout the area stopped by the log cabin.

"I can cure the boy," he promised Billy's mother. With a secret remedy, the doctor mixed mulberry leaves, elderberries and other wild fruits into a paste. From that day forward, Billy began to grow stronger. Soon, Billy played and began to run faster than any of the other boys his age. The healing from berries is something Sunday never forgot. For the

Billy began to grow stronger.

rest of his life, Sunday continued to eat elderberries and mulberries and drink sassafras tea. He claimed that nature had a plant for any illness.

"Where's Billy?" Jennie wondered about her three-year-old son. Only a few days earlier, Billy's grandmother had died in midwinter. They attended the funeral in a small graveyard. From the front of the cabin, they could almost see the grave. Now, in the snow, Jennie followed her small son's footprints. She watched from a distance as Billy knelt in the snow at his grandmother's grave. He prayed a little prayer that his mother had taught him.

"Hey, boy, how would you like a job?" a neighborhood farmer smiled as he looked down from his wagon at Billy Sunday. At seven years old, Billy had never worked. To help the farmer would be his first job. For the next eight days, the farmer hitched a four-horse team to a reaper. Billy drove the horses

At seven years old, Billy had never worked.

and earned twenty-five cents a day.

At the end of the eight days, Billy struggled to walk down the road toward home. Every part of his little body was sore from driving the horses. His eyes hurt from the hours in the bright sun. "Wait until I show Momma," he thought. The money almost burned in his pocket—a two dollar bill.

After Billy showed the money to his mother, she turned and said, "And I've got something for you." To his amazement, Billy tried on his first hickory shirt. While he worked, his mother had made the shirt.

"Thank you Momma," Billy said. On impulse, Billy knew how to spend his money from the job. Several months earlier, his half-sister, Elizabeth, had suddenly died in an accident. His mother had a small picture of her child. Billy took his two dollars and had the picture enlarged then framed.

Billy had the picture enlarged then framed.

BILLY SUNDAY

As a boy, Billy faced many hard experiences. One day, a horse kicked his older brother, Albert in the head. He never recovered and eventually went to a mental hospital. Billy felt the loss of his brother and the deaths of his half-sister and father along with his own struggle with sickness. His early days were filled with fear and uncertainty.

One of Billy's heroes growing up was his Grand-father Squire. This old man could build wagons or houses or stone walls. He even built a mill to make sugar cane into sugar.

"Billy, hold out your hands and balance," Grand-father said. On the back of a bareback horse, Billy Sunday slowly stood. In the hours grandfather and grandson spent together, Billy learned gymnastics and horseback riding. Squire would ride his horse into the town of Ames with Billy sitting proudly on his shoulders. Sunday became very skilled at

"Billy, hold out your hands and balance."

different tricks. Once a visiting local circus asked Billy to join them, but the boy refused.

During the school year, Billy sat on rough benches in a small one room school house. He learned reading, writing and arithmetic from the neighborhood teachers.

One day, Billy was out pulling weeds in his grandfather's garden. He worked on one row while Grandfather worked on another one. For a while, Billy kept up with his grandfather. While tugging on the weeds, Billy enjoyed the breezy day. It was a great day for fishing. Soon his thoughts soared about two miles away to the nearby pond.

His grandfather was busy pulling weeds and didn't notice his "helper." Finally, Grandfather stretched and looked around for Billy. To his surprise, Billy was sitting under a shaded bush.

"Hello, son, what are you doing here?" the old

Billy was sitting under a shaded bush.

gentleman asked.

"I was just a-thinking, Grandfather," Billy said.

"Thinking? Thinking about what?" he asked.

"I'm thinking when I get to be a man, I'm not going to pull weeds," Billy said with conviction. "I'm going to hunt around and find a good job where I can work with my head."

Billy's grandfather just shook his head. "Wonder if that boy is going to do any good when he is grown up?" Time revealed an amazing story.

"Drunk again?" Billy thought. The twelve-year-old walked into his cabin home and looked over at the sleeping figure of Leroy Heizer, his stepfather. "How could our mother trust this man with our family?" He slammed the door of the cabin and walked away. He headed toward his grandfather's house nearby.

Before long Leroy Heizer packed his bags and

"Thinking? Thinking about what?"

disappeared. His struggle with alcohol had been lost. Heizer abandoned Jennie and their children. Once again, Billy's mother was alone with her children and without any money. Still in her early thirties, Jennie made a hard decision.

"Boys," she told her sons, "I'm going to send you to the Soldiers' Orphan's Home in Glenwood." The official name was the Iowa State Orphan's Asylum but most people called it the "Soldiers' Home." During the Civil War, these homes were organized to care for the children of soldiers who had died on the battlefields and hospitals.

It was a sad day when the two boys left their farm and traveled into town. They had to take the train from Ames to Glenwood, which was 150 miles away. Billy had never been more than eight miles from his family cabin. They waited in a small hotel near the train station. At one in the morning, Jennie

Jennie made a hard decision.

woke her boys. "Get ready. The train is coming."

When the boys looked into their mother's face, they saw her eyes were red from weeping and her cheeks were wet from the tears. Jennie Sunday only had enough money for two tickets to Council Bluffs, Iowa. She didn't have enough money for the boys to reach Glenwood.

When they arrived at the Ames train station, Jennie put one arm around Billy and the other around Edward. With her head down, she sobbed as if her heart was breaking. People headed to the train streamed around the trio. Jennie knew that she wouldn't see her boys again for several years.

As the boys settled into seats on the train, their mother stood on the station platform. Through her tears, she was smiling. "Good-bye," Billy said through the window. It marked his first good-bye to his mother. As the train pulled out, the boys knew

"Good-bye."

their mother loved and cared for them.

Early in the morning, the train pulled into Council Bluffs. Billy and Edward shivered in the cold air and turned their coat collars up around their necks. The boys saw a sign for a little hotel and began to walk towards it. They stopped a woman on the street and asked for something to eat.

"What are your names?" the woman asked.

"My name is Billy Sunday," the small boy said with firmness, "and this is my brother, Ed."

As she looked over the boys and their small bag, she asked, "Where are you going?"

"To the Soldiers' Orphan's Home at Glenwood," Billy said. Suddenly, tears came to the woman's eyes and she said, "My husband was a soldier, but he never came back from the war. He never turned anyone away from our door and I surely won't turn you boys away." With her arms outstretched, the

"I surely won't turn you boys away."

woman said, "Come on in." She gave the boys breakfast and lunch.

The boys played near the freight trains until the train for Burlington arrived. As the train began to move, they climbed on the caboose. After several minutes, the conductor came and asked, "Where are your tickets?"

"Ain't got any," Billy answered.

"Where's your money?" the conductor said.

"Ain't got any," came the reply.

Shaking his head, the conductor said, "Then I'll have to put you off at the next station." Both boys broke out in tears. Ed handed the conductor a letter of introduction to the superintendent of the Orphan's Home. While reading the letter, the man's eyes filled with tears. "Just sit still boys. It won't cost you a cent to ride my train. It's twenty miles from Council Bluffs to Glenwood."

"Where's your money?"

When the boys rounded the corner, the conductor shouted to them, "Boys, the home is up there on the hill." Sunday never forgot the kindness of the trainman.

Sunday never forgot the kindness of the trainman.

"You're really fast, Billy!"

2

A Growing Independence

"Edward, let's go exploring," Billy encouraged his brother at the Glenwood Home. The boys had only been there for a few days. The home was pretty isolated from the town and had plenty of thick forests and rolling meadows to explore. Billy and Ed would chase rabbits and squirrels. Sometimes they would play baseball with the other boys or organize foot races.

"You're really fast, Billy!" John exclaimed to his new friend. To John's surprise, Billy won every single foot race. Nobody in the school could match Billy's speed on foot.

"That bully keeps on causing trouble," James said to Billy and five other boys at Glenwood. "It's got to come to a stop but it will take all of us."

For weeks, Billy had watched the stockily built Sam secretly hit smaller boys and make these boys run errands for him. For the first time, Billy saw how the strong overtook the weak in his world. He wanted it to stop.

"Yeah, count me in," Billy said. "We'll teach him a lesson that he won't forget." Then Billy told the group of five how they could teach Sam a lesson. Every one knew that fighting was against the rules of the school, but several nights later, they "dared the bully to come outside."

At about 3:00 a.m., a dozen boys poured out of the school. They climbed down windows and drainpipes. The group gathered over at a small clump of trees a safe and quiet distance from the

The group gathered over at a small clump of trees.

school building.

In the dim light, they formed a ring and the bully went into the center saying, "Who wants to take me on tonight?"

"I will," Billy said. The bully laughed at the small–sized boy.

"Then you're asking for it," Sam sneered.

In a moment, the tables turned. Billy got in the first punch and then a series of blows planted firmly on Sam's fat face. The other boys laughed as Billy danced with the agility of a cat. Finally Sam the bully got what he deserved. The next day, he had a completely different attitude around the school. The boys began looking to Sunday as a leader.

Discipline was something that Billy was forced to learn at the Glenwood Home. If a student didn't promptly arrive for a meal, they missed that meal and the next meal. Billy had a hard time learning to

Finally Sam the bully got what he deserved.

obey this rule. As a growing boy, when Billy missed
two meals, it began to show. His older brother, Ed
worried about his thin brother. "How can I help
Billy get his food?" Ed wondered. "Perfect! I'll
work in the kitchen!" Soon Ed was assigned to clean
and lock the kitchen. He performed his duty faith-
fully but always managed to sneak a plate of food
into a convenient corner. With Edward's help, in
spite of his late arrival at meals, Billy began to fill
out and grow strong.

On the first day of the week, Sunday often went
to a revival meeting. Throughout his years in
Glenwood, Billy and Ed attended the revival meetings. They enjoyed the singing and the action. Little
did Billy know that these tent meetings would grow
in importance in his own future.

After a year and a half in Glenwood, the home
was suddenly closed. Sixty boys, including the

"Perfect! I'll work in the kitchen!"

Sunday brothers, were transferred to the Davenport Home in Davenport, Iowa. In his new environment, Billy gained good schooling along with some religious instruction. The teachers inspired their students to achieve and be something in this world.

The Davenport Home spread over sixty acres of land and included several buildings. S.W. Pierce and his wife ran the home. They were a polished team, with Mr. Pierce as the enforcer and symbol of authority. In contrast, his wife was the nurturing shepherd who displayed caring and comfort to the boys under their care. Mr. Pierce demanded careful grooming, respect and order—something that Billy didn't appreciate at the time but learned the importance of later in his life.

One day Mr. Pierce looked around the school for Billy Sunday. "Has anyone seen Billy Sunday?" Mr. Pierce asked. "Edward, where is your brother?"

"Edward, where is your brother?"

The older Sunday shrugged his shoulders. Billy had run away. Pierce had a reputation with runaways. He chased them across Iowa until he found them and returned them home. Whether by foot, horseback or train, Mr. Pierce chased the boys in his care. Now it was Billy's turn for the chase.

Sunday didn't get far before Mr. Pierce returned him to the Home. "Ok, Billy, you know the punishment," Mr. Pierce said. For the next eight weeks, Billy marched around the cinder track in front of the school's administration building. He circled the track for eight hours a day with breaks only for meals or sleep. He would think twice about running away from the Davenport Home again.

The Home required each boy to work. Billy made beds, scrubbed floors, washed laundry or dishes and worked on the school's farm. Also, the Pierces required academic excellence and required that

"Ok, Billy, you know the punishment."

Billy read his religious readings each night in front of the other boys. Since rules were rules, Billy endured the discipline of the Home, but he didn't like it.

After several years, Edward turned sixteen. He was required to leave the home. About this time, Billy announced to the Pierces, "I'm not staying here without Ed. I'm leaving too."

Billy's mother and grandfather agreed, and both brothers returned to their home in Ames, Iowa. Jennie Sunday had moved out of the family log cabin and into her father's home. The two boys had become independent in their time away from home. Before long, Ed moved with a neighbor. After several years, Ed returned to Davenport and worked as a carpenter and watchman at the Home.

Grandfather Squire was someone Billy admired. If anyone came to their door hungry, the generous

"I'm leaving too."

old man never turned anyone away. His grandfather was almost like a father to Billy. One day Billy came to his grandfather, "The spelling match will soon begin. My friend John has a white store collar that's going to help him. Do you think I could have a white collar, Grandfather?"

"Listen to me, son," the old man said. "It's not what you wear on you, but what you have in you that makes you a man. Be honest, and do your work with all your might, and then some day you won't have to wear a white collar to make folks look up to you."

Billy decided that he didn't need a white collar for the spelling match. For many years, he held on to this idea about the importance of what's inside rather than outside. He never forgot the lesson.

In many ways, life on the farm made Billy restless. Often Sunday felt that he was stuck and

"Listen to me, son."

needed to move on with his life. One day his thoughts turned into action. With his half-brother LeRoy, Billy was hitching a team of horses. Grandfather Squire was anxious to get to town. While the old man danced on one leg and then the other, suddenly the large ring on the yoke for the horses broke. Like their grandfather, both boys were surprised. The broken yoke was too much for the old man.

"You clumsy, no good boys," Grandfather began. He hurled insults for several minutes. Sunday received a tongue lashing that he never forgot.

"If that's the way you feel, then I'm leaving," Billy announced. Impulsively, the fourteen-year-old packed his bags and left Ames. He never lived at home again.

After staying with a nearby friend for several days, Sunday went to Nevada, Iowa which was eight

"If that's the way you feel, then I'm leaving."

miles away. For a few weeks, Billy worked as an errand boy in a small hotel. He met the trains and carried baggage and did other odd jobs. He returned home to ease the tension with his family, but after a few days went back to Nevada.

In Nevada, Sunday learned that Colonel John Scott, once the lieutenant-governor of Iowa, wanted to hire a boy. Billy knocked on the front door and asked for the job. After a brief talk with Sunday, the Colonel almost offered Billy the job.

"I'm not so sure about this," Mrs. Scott said. "You can go and scrub my cellar steps for me, son." As Billy walked toward the steps, his face was covered with a large smile. Scrubbing steps was one of his specialities from the years at the Soldier's Home. Billy thoroughly cleaned the steps from top to bottom. He got the job in the Scott home.

Among his various duties, Billy cared for twenty

He got the job in the Scott home.

Shetland ponies. He earned eight dollars a month along with his room and board. Concerned about his education, the Scotts arranged for Sunday to attend public school. To get educated out on the Iowa prairie wasn't easy, but Nevada High School had a growing reputation for excellence in academics and preparing their students for college.

Billy had plenty of energy and drive. Besides working for the Scotts and attending school, Sunday became a part-time janitor at the high school. Through the winter months, Billy got out of bed at 2 a.m. and slogged to school. He started fires in 14 different stoves in the school then swept and cleaned the school before the other students arrived. He showed a characteristic which followed him throughout his life—high energy and strength to endure practically anything.

"Hurry, Robert," Susan said to her classmate.

Sunday became a part-time janitor at the high school.

"We've got to get to the school assembly. Billy Sunday is speaking again and we don't want to miss a single word." As the students assembled, a nervous Billy was pacing behind the stage curtain. His hands shook as he looked over his notes.

After his introduction, Billy began to talk about the classic poem, "Parrhasius and the Captive" by Nathaniel Parker Willis. He told about this poem in which a man is captured and tortured, then a Greek artist paints the agony of the moment. Sunday didn't just speak about the poem. He punctuated his talk with moans and cries for help. Then, at one dramatic moment, Sunday reached behind the podium and lifted out some clanking chains. All of the students and teachers were spellbound watching Billy's speaking skills. His talks soared in popularity so that when a student speech was announced, the first question was, "Is Billy Sunday

The students and teachers were spellbound.

speaking?" If the answer was "yes," then a large audience filled the auditorium.

Beyond Sunday's speaking abilities, his fellow students at Nevada High were amazed at his quick running skills. One day a cocky young man walked into Nevada High and challenged anyone to a foot-race. "I'll run against you," Billy said. They lined up at the corner and someone started the race. Soon the out–of–town boy was left behind in Billy's dust. No one could run faster than Sunday.

The town of Ames buzzed with excitement about their Fourth of July celebration. The red, white and blue colors of America were scattered throughout the town. Lemonade was made in a large under-ground container and sold for a nickel a glass. Street vendors sold firecrackers. There was music in the street and games.

One of the most popular events was the hundred-

The out—of—town boy was left behind in Billy's dust.

yard dash. Many people trained for the running event. One summer, Billy Sunday decided to enter the race. The winner would earn a three–dollar cash prize.

As the contestants lined up for the race, the crowd had a favorite. A local college professor had a rose–colored running suit and running shoes. Thirteen men and one teenager lined up at the starting line. Billy removed his shirt and turned up his overalls. The crowd began to talk—Billy was barefoot. At twenty-five yards, the runners were in a group. Then at fifty yards, three runners surged ahead—the professor, a farmer and Billy. As the crowd roared, they came closer to the finish line. At seventy-five yards, the farmer had dropped behind. Billy ran shoulder with the college professor. Five yards before the finish line, Billy ran ahead and crossed before the professor.

Billy crossed before the professor.

BILLY SUNDAY

"Hurrah for Sunday," his friends shouted as they hoisted Billy on their shoulders. He treated his friends to lemonade and ice cream with his prize winnings. It was an unforgettable foot race.

"Hurrah for Sunday."

"I'm moving to the city."

3

Play Ball

"Marshalltown," one of Billy's friends said to him. "Why you moving there?"

Sunday was packing his belongings. "I'm giving up on the country and moving to the city. Besides, the Marshalltown Fire Brigade wants me to work with them."

Fire departments in the late 1800s were volunteers. They regularly competed with other fire departments to see who would be the first to arrive at the fires. Marshalltown had learned of Sunday's quick running ability. His running became Sunday's key to leaving the farm and moving to a different life.

BILLY SUNDAY

Two months before his eighteenth birthday, Sunday moved thirty miles east to the growing community which was turning into a small city. Billy got a job in a furniture shop which also had an funeral home business. Billy did everything from assembling and varnishing chairs to making coffins to driving horses to the grave yard. Immediately, he took a dislike to the job. For him, it almost equaled how much he hated farming. One of his least favorite jobs was varnishing chairs.

One day the shop owner watched him work on some chairs. He stopped Billy and said, "Here let me show you how to do it." Then the man gave the furniture several strokes from his brush. Turning to Sunday he said, "Can't you do it like that?"

"Not on your life," Billy said, "or I wouldn't be working for you for three dollars a week."

The furniture business did permit Sunday to play

Billy did everything.

baseball with the Marshalltown team. He immediately gained a following because of his quick speed. He was known for stealing bases and his play in the outfield. The team won many games throughout the region. By the end of the 1882 season, they had defeated every team in eastern Iowa, and people said they were Iowa's best. Word about the team reached the capital, Des Moines. The city fathers in Des Moines challenged the Marshalltown players to play their undefeated team. Sunday's team rose to the challenge. Some people on the side bet $500 on the game to the winners.

Late in the summer, the Marshalltown team traveled 90 miles to Des Moines. Some of the local people also made the trip. Billy was one of the stars of the game, which they won 15 to 6. Unknown to Billy, his Aunt Em was in the crowd. An avid fan of the Marshalltown team, Aunt Em had a nephew,

Billy was one of the stars of the game.

Adrian Anson, the captain and manager of the Chicago White Stockings. During the off season, Adrian (Cap) Anson lived in Mashalltown. While he tried to get away from baseball throughout the winter of 1882, Aunt Em graphically re-told stories about the baseball skills of Billy Sunday. But Cap never committed to giving Sunday a tryout despite his aunt's urgings.

Then that spring when he assembled the team, Cap invited Sunday to Chicago so he could see this young man for himself. "Come to Chicago for a try–out with the White Stockings," read the telegraph from Anson to Sunday. "We meet at the A.G. Spaulding's Sporting Goods Store at 108 Madison Avenue." Billy's hands shook with excitement. It was his first telegraph. And the White Stockings were one of the top teams in the National Baseball League.

Billy's hands shook with excitement.

With an incredible self-confidence, Sunday quit his job and took out his entire savings of six dollars. He purchased a sage-green suit. From a friend, Sunday borrowed $4.50 and spent $3.50 on the train trip to Chicago. He arrived with a dollar in his pocket.

Chicago was only 250 miles from Marshalltown, Iowa but to Billy it was like going to another world. The second largest city in the United States, Chicago had tall buildings that reached even nine floors. Many of these buildings were made from brick or stone. They were completely different from the wooden structures of Des Moines. Billy saw massive factories and warehouses.

Within an hour of his arrival in the city, Sunday arrived at the sporting goods shop. A.C. Spaulding owned the White Stockings. He walked up to the door as the factory whistle blew 7:00 a.m. "Where

Sunday arrived at the sporting goods shop.

is everyone?" Most stores in Iowa opened at 7:00 a.m. He sat on the curb and waited an hour until the store opened. Another two hours later, members of the team began to slowly arrive. After a while, Cap Anson strolled into the meeting. The tall, rugged and burly man introduced himself to Sunday. Then Cap said, "Billy, they tell me that you can run some. Fred Pfeffer is our crack runner. How about putting on a little race this morning?"

"I'm ready, sir," Sunday answered. He was eager to quit waiting around and get on with the tryout. His nervousness faded some as he walked with the team to a nearby ballpark. Billy borrowed a uniform from a pitcher on the team but didn't have any baseball shoes.

Pfeffer lined up at the mark with his running shoes and uniform. Sunday wore a huge oversized uniform and no shoes. The two players raced to the

"I'm ready, sir."

finish line. Billy crossed about 15 feet before Pfeffer. It was Billy's speed that impressed Cap Anson and won Sunday a place on the White Stockings team.

After the tryouts, Anson asked Billy, "How are you fixed for money?"

"I have one dollar," Sunday said. Reaching into his pocket, Anson tossed Billy a twenty dollar gold piece. This act of kindness made a lasting impression on Sunday.

During his first season with the White Stockings, Billy only played in fourteen games. He also managed all of the team money for Anson while they were traveling. Billy made all of the hotel and train reservations for the team. Often Billy carried thousands of dollars in his satchel. He was a trusted member of the team.

Later Cap Anson wrote about Sunday's early days

Anson tossed Billy a twenty dollar gold piece.

on the team saying, "The first thirteen times that Sunday went to bat, he struck out. I was convinced that he would make a ball player, and hung on to him, cheering him up as best I could whenever he became discouraged. As a base runner, his judgment was at times faulty. He was altogether too daring, taking extraordinary chances because of the tremendous turn of speed he possessed. He was a good fielder, and a strong and accurate thrower. His weak point was his batting. Sunday in my opinion was the strongest man in the profession on his feet, and could run the bases like a frightened deer."

Sports writers called Sunday the best base runner in the whole league. His picture began to appear on some of the early baseball cards. The White Stockings began to set up races outside of baseball to show off Billy's amazing speed. One day, Cap Anson had set up a hundred yard race

The first thirteen times, he struck out.

against Arlie Latham of the St. Louis Browns. Each side put up $500 and the winner took the gate money for the game.

The race would be held at the end of the season. "I don't want to run that race against Latham," Sunday said one day. He came to Cap Anson and said, "You'll have to let me out of the race."

"Why Billy," he said, "you're not going to be yellow, and a quitter, are you?"

Sunday continued to talk about wanting out of the race but Anson wouldn't hear of it.

"No, Billy," Cap explained. "I've backed you for a thousand dollars in this race, and so have a lot of my friends. There's about seventy-five thousand dollars riding on this race. You go down to St. Louis and run like the wind."

Sunday didn't have much choice. He lined up at the marks against Latham. As always, Billy won the race by a large margin.

"I've backed you for a thousand dollars in this race."

BILLY SUNDAY

Baseball in 1886 was a rough game. Sunday didn't fit the typical image of a baseball player. Most players were heavy drinkers of alcohol and endured weeks of travel on the road to games. Often during these early years of baseball, the players would have fist fights with the umpires over decisions. Sometimes the players traded verbal barbs with the fans. At times fights broke out between players and fans. Billy Sunday stood apart as a clean-cut and innocent kid from the plains of Iowa. He had a reputation for hard work and a dedication to his team.

While Sunday did go into the bars and drink with his teammates, Billy never got out of control. During those times when Billy was tempted to drink too much, he remembered his mother singing hymns in his log cabin or Mrs. Pierce from the Davenport Home telling Bible stories. He drew comfort from the simple faith of his friends and family on the Iowa prairie.

Billy Sunday stood apart as an innocent kid.

Sunday was beginning to feel drunk.

4

I'm Through

The summer weather in June 1886 was perfect for
baseball. Billy Sunday and his teammates were at
home in Chicago for a series against the New York
Giants. Along with several Giants players, the men
were drinking alcohol at their favorite bars. Sunday was beginning to feel drunk and light–headed
from the alcohol. When they walked past the
corner of State and Van Buren Streets, the group sat
down for a few minutes on the curb side. There
was a show worth watching across the street. A
"Gospel Wagon" with a team of horses was filled
with men and women. With trumpets, flutes and a

trombone, they filled the air with music from hymns. The music reminded Billy of his days as a child when his mother sang hymns in their log cabin home in Iowa. Sunday began to cry as he thought about the music.

One of the men from the Pacific Garden Mission noticed how Sunday reacted to the music. He walked over to Billy and the other players. "Won't you come to our service. It's only two blocks away," Harry Monroe said to Billy. "You'll hear some things that will interest you."

Something stirred deep inside Billy. In some ways, he looked like a man with everything in life. In a single month with the White Stockings, he earned more money than a year on the farm. In his third season of baseball, Billy was popular with the crowd and a successful athlete. But inside, Billy felt empty. He wanted something more in his life.

He wanted something more in his life.

Billy stood and told his teammates, "Boys, I bid the old life good-by."

Some of the players laughed. Others smiled. Still others shrugged their shoulders and had a look of admiration mixed with disgust. Sunday and the clean-shaven young man walked to the Mission. The building for the service wasn't fancy. In fact, it was located in between a couple of bars and dance halls. Over the door a sign said, "Strangers Welcome." Another wall held a verse from 1 Timothy 1:15 in the Bible which says, "Christ came into the world to save sinners, among whom I am chief."

Billy walked into the Mission and sat down among homeless men and drunks. Harry Moore began the service. After several hymns, a number of men stood and told how Christ had changed their lives. Some were former burglars. Others had been caught in alcohol but now they were freed through

"Boys, I bid the old life good-by."

the power of Christ. Sunday sat among the shabbily-dressed audience and carefully listened to the message.

When the invitation was extended for those in the audience to commit their life to Christ, Sunday didn't move from his chair. "I'll be coming back again to this Mission," he resolved as he returned home.

During the next five nights, Sunday attended the services at the Mission. One night, Sunday knew he needed to commit his life to Christ, but he felt like he couldn't do it alone.

A nervous Billy stood up and knocked down several of the curved-backed wooden chairs. Some people nearby assumed that Sunday had been drinking alcohol. In reality, Sunday's mind was clear. Billy had a life-changing decision to make.

Others walked to the front during the singing.

"I'll be coming back again to this Mission."

Sunday stood and tried to decide about walking forward. Suddenly Mrs. Clarke came and placed her arms around him. The wife of Colonel George R. Clarke, a western miner and Chicago businessman, Mrs. Clarke whispered to Sunday, "God loves you. Jesus died for you, and he wants you to love him and give your heart to him."

The ball player could no longer resist. He swung clumsily around the chairs and walked to a seat in the front near the stage. Henry Monroe came beside Billy and they knelt to pray. Mrs. Clarke joined the two men in prayer.

"I want to make that commitment tonight," Billy said. He bowed his head and accepted Christ. Mrs. Clarke told Billy some verses from the Bible and urged him to obey God's commands.

Years later, Sunday wrote about his decision during that night. He said, "I have followed Jesus from

He bowed his head and accepted Christ.

that day to this every second, like the hound on the trail of the fox."

Immediately Billy experienced several changes in his life. First, Billy felt relieved from the guilt about his past. A great emotional burden lifted off the shoulders of the young baseball player. Also Billy felt like his life might be moving in a different direction.

The next day, Sunday wondered how his teammates would react to his decision about Jesus. Every morning the White Stockings players arrived at their ball park for practice. Sunday expected to be ridiculed and laughed out of the team.

As Sunday opened his locker to change into his clothes, his teammate, Mike Kelly came over and said, "Billy, I'm proud of you." With a large smile on his face, he continued, "Religion ain't my strong suit, but I'll help you all I can." The others on the

"Billy, I'm proud of you."

team came and congratulated Sunday for his decision. Not a single player laughed at Sunday for going to the Mission.

Before long, the Chicago team left for St. Louis. Sunday refused to go with his teammates to the bars and to gamble away his spare time. Instead, Sunday located a used bookstore. He found a Bible in the shop.

"How much for this book?" he asked the shop keeper. For thirty-five cents, Sunday left with the book. He immediately began reading. Sunday wanted to locate those promises and commands from God that Mrs. Clarke had told him about.

In one game, the White Stockings were playing Detroit. The two teams were tied for the championship, and only four more games were left in the season. Sunday was playing right field.

It was the last inning and the White Stockings

"How much for this book?"

were ahead. Two men were out and a Detroit player was on second base and another was on third. The batter had three balls and two strikes. Sunday called to John G. Clarkson, the White Stockings pitcher, "One more, John and we've got them!"

Clarkson wound up for the pitch and just as he was about to throw, his foot slipped. The ball went low instead of high. The Detroit batter swung hard at the ball and cracked it. Sunday looked and knew the ball was headed into the overflowing crowd. Some of the fans were seated on the edges of the outfield.

"Get out of the way!" Billy yelled into the crowd. The crowd opened like the Red Sea was parting. Billy flew towards where the ball would land and prayed quickly, "O Lord, if you ever helped a man, help me get that ball!" Sunday stuck his glove into the air and the ball hit it. He fell back from the

"O Lord, help me get that ball!"

impact but managed to hold onto it.

The White Stockings fans went wild with excitement. The game was over. Tom Johnson, former mayor of Cleveland, rushed up to Sunday and poked a ten dollar bill into his hand. "Here, Billy," he cried. "Greatest thing I ever saw! Buy yourself the best hat in Chicago on me!"

Besides reading his Bible, Billy joined the Chicago Central YMCA Bible Training Class and began to study through the entire Bible. Also Sunday began attending the Jefferson Park Presbyterian Church on Chicago's West Side. The church was near his rented room and also not far from the West Side Ball Park where the White Stockings played their home games.

While on the road with the team, Billy attended church services. Once in Allegheny, Pennsylvania, the church asked Sunday to teach a Sunday school

Billy began to study through the entire Bible.

class. He readily agreed. As Billy began the class, the young men in the class started asking many baseball questions.

Sunday raised his hand to stop the questions and said, "Fellows, tomorrow if you come around the hotel, I'll be glad to tell you all I can about baseball. But I can't do it today. This is God's day and I'm here to do his work best I can. Let's see what we can get out of this lesson."

There were no more baseball questions. With great attention, the class listened to the young man.

Sunday continued to play baseball for the next five years. As he traveled with the team, he gave religious talks in various cities. Primarily, Sunday spoke in the Young Men's Christian Associations. As the word spread about the baseball player turned Christian, churches began to invite Sunday to speak at their services.

He gave religious talks in various cities.

As an eastern newspaper reported about Sunday, "It's something of a novelty to see a professional ball player get up in a pulpit. Forget about base hits, home runs, brilliant catches. For a while Sunday told the great doctrines of Christ with such force that it brought tears to the eyes of over 1500 people."

A Pittsburgh newspaper also reported about the young baseball player saying, "William A. Sunday has a ready command of the English language. His knowledge of human nature and the Scriptures were clearly evident in the half-hour address at the YMCA yesterday afternoon. He made no reference to baseball and his words were well-chosen."

At first, people were drawn to hear Billy Sunday the professional baseball player. When they heard Billy, the crowds were captivated by his public speaking. Also Billy made the Bible come alive in an understandable way. He received more invita-

"Sunday told the great doctrines of Christ with force ."

tions to speak.

Throughout this time, Sunday continued attending Jefferson Park Presbyterian Church. One evening a friend introduced Billy to Helen Amelia Thompson. Eighteen-year-old Helen, or Nell, stood about five feet four inches and had raven black hair and eyes. Immediately, Billy was in love. He thought, "There's a swell girl." The Thompson family were respected members of the church and the local society. Nell's father owned and operated a prominent dairy factory in Chicago.

After thinking about it for several weeks, Billy got the courage to ask Nell, "Could I see you at your home?" At first, Nell considered saying no but then she said, "Yes." While Nell was interested in Sunday, she was already steadily dating another man. Nell tried to interest Billy in one of her best friends, but he wasn't interested.

Immediately, Billy was in love.

Thoughts of Nell were constantly in Billy's mind. He devised a plan to win her heart. At the next prayer meeting, Billy sat with one eye on the preacher and one eye on Nell. That night Sunday's plan didn't work because Nell's boyfriend sat down next to Nell at the service. Then one night, the boyfriend didn't show. With unusual swiftness, Sunday moved to sit beside Nell.

"Can I walk you home tonight after the meeting," Sunday said, almost begging. Nell agreed. Her house was only about a hundred yards from the church.

Billy knew he had to see more of Nell—but how? He changed his route to baseball practice and walked past her home every day that the team was in Chicago. He'd walk past the Thompson home for the ten o'clock practice. Then he'd swing past again when he returned home for lunch. If the team had a

Sunday moved to sit beside Nell.

3:45 game or another practice, Sunday circled past the Thompson home. The return from the practice made four opportunities to see Nell.

One day, Billy figured his plan was working. At each of his four walks past Nell's house, she had been sweeping her front steps and sidewalk. Sometimes if the game went long, Nell swept until Billy came along. She showed great interest in the games—who won and how Billy played. Eventually Nell broke off with her boyfriend and began to date Billy.

On New Year's Eve 1888, Sunday proposed marriage to Nell. Immediately, she accepted. When Billy walked home that night, he said, "I felt like I had wings on my feet. I didn't sleep that night. Visions of Nell's black eyes stared at me from the darkness and turned my night into day."

The next day, Nell's father raged in the Thomp-

Sunday proposed marriage to Nell.

son home. "No daughter of mine will marry a base-ball player," he said. "Even if he happens to be religious and give lectures at the Y.M.C.A. These men are undependable." Nell refused to listen to her father's warnings. The couple planned a fall wedding date.

In the middle of the 1888 season, Sunday was called into A.G. Spaulding's office. "Billy, we've traded you to Pittsburgh. I wish you well," Spaulding said. There was no discussion. In shock, Sunday packed his bags to begin playing for the Pittsburgh Alleghanies.

His time away from Nell was heartbreaking. During the spring and summer, Sunday wrote Nell daily. "I keep your photo in my Bible," he wrote. "So I will see it each time I open the Scriptures." In his daily letters, Billy wrote of loneliness and self-pity. His moods seemed to swing when he attended

"Billy, we've traded you to Pittsburgh."

church on Sunday and Wednesday evenings.

Nell noticed the pattern and wrote back, "Everybody likes you and appreciates you. Now brace up and throw off that burden that pulls you down and be the strong, stout-hearted man that you are." She told about how her father often traveled but never had this continual loneliness. "Stop it right now," she said. "Your body will have to give way to your mind and brain fever will result." She ended with a bit of an apology, "I had to write this. I can't go on."

Sunday got the message. In reply, Sunday wrote a loving and positive letter to Nell. His baseball began to improve and his letters turned positive. The lesson about loneliness was important to Billy and Nell because of their future life together. The separations would be many.

After a Pittsburgh game against Indianapolis,

"Stop it right now."

Billy boarded a train for Chicago. The next day, Nell and Billy were married on September 5, 1888 at two in the afternoon. Immediately after the ceremony, the couple attended a Chicago White Stockings baseball game. A.G. Spaulding, his former boss, draped a box with decorations and the crowd gave the new couple a standing ovation.

At five o'clock Billy and Nell left on the Pennsylvania Limited. The next day, in Pittsburgh, Sunday started a game in left field for the Pittsburgh Alleghanies. Nell and Billy began a life together which would have many long separations.

Nell and Billy were married on September 5, 1888.

"Boys can you stop playing poker?"

5

Preacher in Training

"Boys can you stop playing poker?" Billy asked his surprised teammates. "After all it is the sabbath." Only minutes before, Sunday had strutted to the back of the train car as the members of the Pittsburgh Alleghanies traveled to their next game. The other players scrambled to hide their cards and act like their game was over.

Billy returned to his seat in the front of the car. He turned to another teammate, Bob Allen, and said, "Well, I made 'em stop. But please don't go back there and see how long they remained stopped." With a large grin, Billy continued, "I know that bunch. But they'll realize I'm right some day."

Sunday sat down and began to read his Bible. While some players read or relaxed looking out the window, Billy worked with his Bible and notebook. If he found a Bible phrase that interested him, Billy wrote it in his notebook. Later with the noise of the train in the background, Sunday would practice using these phrases in a speech. Throughout the National Baseball League, players believed that Sunday was bound to become a preacher.

In between his baseball games and during the off season, Billy took many classes in subjects like physics and English. Although he never graduated from a college, these courses helped him later in his career. At the YMCA, Billy gave talks to young people about religion and personal habits.

"Billy Sunday's going to be here," said one excited boy. "He was one of the best players on the

"Billy Sunday's going to be here."

White Stockings but they traded him to Pittsburgh."
The young men flocked to the centers so they could
hear Sunday. One of his first speeches was entitled,
"The Earnestness in the Christian Life." A local
newspaper reporter wrote about the speech, "If W.
A. Sunday plays ball as well and as earnestly as he
talked yesterday before a large body of men in the
hall of the Young Men's Christian Association, he
ought to be in great demand among rival clubs."
Sunday's popularity as a speaker continued to grow.

The leaders at the YMCA watched Sunday take
additional study courses in Bible. One day the director of the Central Association in Chicago came
to Sunday with an offer, "We'd like you to be the
Secretary of our Religious Department." After ex-
plaining the responsibilities of the job, he looked
down with a bit of sadness, "And we'll only be able
to pay you eighty-three dollars a month."

"We'll only be able to pay you eighty-three dollars a month."

Sunday practically jumped at the chance to work for the YMCA—even though he was earning several hundred dollars a month as a professional baseball player. "I've got a problem in accepting the position," Billy said. "I've still got my contract with Pittsburgh."

During the 1890 season with Pittsburgh, Sunday played with a group of poor baseball players from around the National League. The team was in last place racking up 113 defeats. One losing streak lasted for 23 straight games. Through the entire season, they won only 28 games.

During one game against Philadelphia, the Pittsburgh team got so desperate, the manager asked Sunday to pitch. Normally an outfielder, Sunday went to the pitching mound during the fifth inning. His first player was walked, the second batter knocked a triple. The third batter hit a double and

Sunday went to the pitching mound.

the fourth player was hit by a pitch. Enough was enough. Sunday returned to his position in center field.

The Pittsburgh team played so poorly that one game only twenty fans watched. One reporter joked, "Sunday can draw more people to a religious talk at the YMCA than the Pittsburgh team can draw to a game."

At the end of the 1890 season, Pittsburgh changed their name from the Alleghanies to the Pirates. But Billy never got a chance to wear the Pirates uniform. He was sold to Philadelphia and signed a three-year contract with the Phillies for 1891 to 1893. As Billy told Nell, "From the minute I signed the contract, I felt it was a wrong decision." With great pain, the couple wondered how to mix Sunday's baseball career with his religious service.

One spring afternoon, Billy and Nell were talk-

"I felt it was a wrong decision."

ing about their future. Billy said, "I know the money that Philadelphia is offering me is more than I've ever made in Pittsburgh or Chicago," he paused, "but I feel like the Lord is calling me to full time Christian work. Three years looks like a long time to me as I think about it. If you don't mind, I would like to send a request for my release."

But Nell did mind! Since the early days of their relationship, Sunday had easily spent money. While Billy never drank or gambled away his money after he became a Christian, he knew nothing about how to save or take care of money. Nell's father was a Chicago businessman and from her family, Nell had learned to be careful with money.

"Maybe these three years in baseball is a gift from God," Nell said. "It would allow us to care for your brother Albert or your mother or our daughter, Helen." Despite her concerns about Billy's changes,

"I would like to send a request for my release."

she didn't want to put money ahead of God in her life. Finally she told Billy, "If this is a call from God, then ask for a release from the Phillies. I'll admit the Lord isn't talking with me about it but if he's talking with you pay attention."

The next day, Sunday telegrammed Philadelphia and asked for a release. The next day came an immediate answer from the baseball executives— "No."

Despite his baseball contract, Billy continued to pray about the job offer. He believed that now it was God's responsibility to arrange his release from baseball.

Later in the spring, Billy met with the baseball executives from the Phillies. "I want out of my contract," he told the men. "I've been offered an important job with the Chicago YMCA."

While patiently listening to their player, the ex-

"I want out of my contract."

ecutives were firm. Sunday had signed a contract to work for the Phillies. A deal was a deal. Billy had to report to spring training. His work continued at the YMCA. In early spring, Billy told the Phillies executives, "I'll not be reporting for spring training. But you can count on my arriving on April first in shape and ready to play. As you know I'd rather be working for the YMCA." The executives told Sunday, "Do what your contract demands."

All spring, Sunday worried about his decision to leave baseball. He loved the game, the competition and the many friendships. He prized the excitement and the opportunity to test his skill again and again. Yet, inside, there was another drive that he couldn't explain. This inner urging drew Sunday toward full-time Christian service.

Sunday couldn't forget his three-year contract with the Phillies. As a Christian, he felt obligated

Sunday worried about his decision to leave baseball.

to play out his contract, but three years seemed like an impossible burden. Finally in prayer, Sunday made a deal with the Lord. He prayed, "Lord, if I don't get my release by March twenty-fifth, I'll take it as an assurance that you want me to play baseball; if I get it before that date I will accept that as evidence that you want me to quit playing ball and go into Christian work."

On March 17, Billy received a letter from Colonel Rogers, president of the Philadelphia Club. He could have his release. The Philadelphia baseball executives decided Billy wouldn't make much of a contribution to the team. His desire to give up baseball had watered down his commitment to the Phillies. They released Sunday from his contract.

Word spread across the baseball community that Billy Sunday was no longer under contract with the Phillies. The Cincinnati Reds made Billy an offer.

They released Sunday from his contract.

"If you play with the Reds in 1891, we'll pay you $5,000," the Cincinnati owner said. That amounted to $500 a month for a seven–month season. It was a hundred dollars more a month than most workers earned in a year.

Sunday could hardly believe his ears. It was five times the amount from the YMCA! Billy couldn't sleep because he was thinking about the money from the Reds. He told a friend, "It loomed like a golden mountain or like the Empire State Building."

The young couple didn't know what to decide. They talked it over with friends at the YMCA and businessmen in Chicago such as Cyrus McCormick, president of McCormick Harvesting Machine Company and president of the YMCA. Many people advised Sunday to play the 1891 season and keep the money, then join the YMCA in the fall. But Nell had another opinion to give Billy. She said,

The young couple didn't know what to decide.

"There is nothing to consider. You promised God to quit."

Billy followed the advice from his wife. He began to work as the Assistant Secretary of the Chicago YMCA and earned $83.33 a month. His baseball days were over. He launched a career in full-time Christian service.

For Billy's work at the YMCA, he had to make many changes in his lifestyle. Often the former major league baseball player went without lunch to save money. He dyed some of his old clothes to make them look new or he wore a plastic collar underneath his shirt to save on dry–cleaning bills.

One day, Billy stood on a street corner in a poor section of Chicago. In an hour of watching, Sunday counted several hundred men going inside one of the bars. Sunday found an old friend from Iowa who worked at a local theater. As his buddy drank

His baseball days were over.

another shot of alcohol, Sunday told the friend about Christ.

"See that bum over there with the torn shoes and pants?" Sunday said. "If you don't change your life's direction and follow Jesus, you're going to be just like that man." His friend from Iowa didn't believe Sunday. He turned back to his drink.

Less than eight months later, Sunday met the same friend on the Chicago streets. Billy could hardly recognize his old friend because of his swollen face and red eyes. "I've lost my job, Billy," the man said. His friend never followed Jesus. Billy walked away shaking his head and thinking, "He's on a toboggan slide heading for hell."

As the secretary at the YMCA, Sunday visited hospitals and courted businessmen for donations. Also he lined up the speakers for the YMCA services and led noon-day prayer meetings and

"He's on a toboggan slide heading for hell."

counseled losers how to be winners.

His daily work on the streets challenged Sunday. He gained a broader perspective on what happened when men and women were consumed with gambling and alcohol. Although Sunday hadn't drunk any alcohol since becoming a Christian, his daily contact with drunks and bums taught some unforgettable lessons. He watched alcohol turn good men into brutes and suck the lifeblood from families. He thought, "I believe whiskey is an evil from hell carrying poverty, death and damnation." This belief became one of the driving forces of his religious zeal for God.

At the YMCA job, Billy followed his call to serve God, but he struggled to pay his bills. A depression hit the country in 1893, and the YMCA had trouble raising money. As their donations dropped, sometimes the YMCA couldn't pay their workers. Billy

"I believe whiskey is an evil from hell."

Sunday's small salary got even smaller.

While Sunday wandered the streets of Chicago for the YMCA, he grew restless. Since his early days in baseball, Billy had traveled from city to city. This traveling filled his need to keep moving. Some of Sunday's time was spent on the streets but many hours were in the headquarters at a desk, buried in paperwork. It was in sharp contrast to the athletic life outside. Sunday felt trapped and his energy was pent up. Less than three years in the job, Sunday quit. In 1894, Billy accepted a position with evangelist John Wilbur Chapman. One of the best known evangelists of his time, Chapman interviewed Sunday during a trip through Chicago.

"We need you to put up tents, sell books, organize committees, and occasionally address meetings," Chapman told the young, eager Sunday. Immediately Billy knew this $40 per-week job was

Sunday felt trapped.

his ticket back to life on the road and the excitement of the crowd. He began his new job with great joy and energy. Unknown to Billy, the change led him closer to his life work.

6

Advance Man

"Song books. Get your song books for the revival," Billy used his loud speaking voice for another purpose. On the road with evangelist J. Wilbur Chapman, Sunday stood outside a tent in a small town outside New York City. Billy was selling song books before Chapman began the service. In only a few months on the road, Billy had become a valued member of the Chapman evangelistic team.

A few years earlier, Chapman had discovered an important aspect of revivals—organization. He became one of the first evangelists to work and plan to draw crowds, coordinate his meeting with many different churches and get advance notice about the meetings. Billy became Chapman's advance man. Several weeks before the dates of the revival, Sunday arrived in a particular town. He helped select the choir members for the music and worked with other men to erect the massive tents. Billy also held meetings with local ministers to gain their support.

While Sunday missed Nell and his children, Billy loved the life on the road. Once again the young Iowan was dizzy in motion. He moved from Paris, Illinois to Troy, New York to Huntington, Pennsylvania. From handling the ropes of the huge tents to leading prayer breakfasts, Billy mastered the method to hold meetings and tell people about Christ. Each city held its own unique problems and challenges, Sunday was charged to pave the way for the evangelist Chapman.

During one of his Chapman's revivals in Indianapolis, Indiana, the crowd buzzed with extra

Billy mastered the method to hold meetings.

excitement. Former President of the United States Benjamin Harrison sat in the audience with his daughter.

"Billy," Chapman said, "go ask President Harrison if he will join us on the platform." Sunday quickly entered the tent and went to the ex-President. "Sir, Mr. Chapman would like you to sit on the platform this evening," Sunday began.

Initially the President held his hands up in protest. The President wanted to remain in the audience. "But Sir," Billy continued. "if you sit on the platform, it will encourage others to take a stand for Christ."

With reluctance, the elderly president agreed and walked down the aisle while holding onto Billy's arm. The crowd was aware of President Harrison and burst into cheers. As the cheers faded, the people began to sing, "My Country 'Tis of Thee." Later,

With reluctance, the elderly president agreed.

Sunday recalled this event as one of his finest moments on the road with Chapman.

Besides doing everything from collecting the offering to selling copies of Chapman's sermons, night after night, Sunday was able to watch the evangelist in action. Chapman had pastored a local church and knew how to listen when he talked with the local ministers. He gained the acceptance of other ministers. Sunday learned from this skilled evangelist.

As Chapman counseled and listened to these local pastors, Sunday understood that these pastors needed their own counselor. Often the success or failure of a revival depended on the local churches. When the local pastors were encouraged, then they could inspire their churches to unite with other churches and reach out to the community.

Besides handling the many details of a crusade

Chapman counseled and listened to these pastors.

for Chapman, Billy gained a practical Bible education from listening to the evangelist. For two years, Billy heard one of the best speakers of his day—Wilbur Chapman. A patient teacher, Chapman gave Billy copies of his sermon notes and outlines. "You've got to clearly present the message of Christ," Chapman said. "But you use stories to make the message practical for the people." Sunday learned how to make his messages ring true to the Bible.

While Billy received instructions from his teacher, Sunday still maintained his distinct speaking skills. No one thought Billy was a copy of Chapman.

Evans hall was packed full with an expectant audience. Evansville, Indiana was preparing for the upcoming meetings of evangelist Chapman. A two-hundred voice choir sat on the platform in front of the audience along with many of the pastors from

ou've got to clearly present the message of Christ."

the city. Among them was Billy Sunday. After the music, Sunday began to speak to the crowd, "The Bible is a common–sense book," he told them. "It shows a man where he stands. It also shows that heaven takes an interest in men. There is no greater joy there than whenever a sinner is saved. Heaven knows how great man's peril has been."

Billy closed his preaching with an earnest prayer. Everyone in the auditorium was standing with their heads bowed. "I'm inviting you to make a commitment to Christ tonight," Sunday said. "Every head is bowed before God. If you'd like to commit your life to Jesus, then raise your hand." Across the room, hands were lifted.

"After we sing the closing song, there will be a short meeting for those who raised their hands," Sunday said. "If you've come with a family, they will wait for you."

Across the room, hands were lifted.

In Paris, Illinois, the crowd had gathered to hear Sunday. The local newspaper editor wrote about the meetings at the Christian Church in the morning and the Presbyterian Church in the afternoon. "Mr. Sunday was the leader at both places. It is evident that his baseball energy has been transferred to his new calling, for he is so much in earnest. It shows in every sentence."

That evening, eighteen hundred people gathered at the large tent outside of the town. Everyone expected Chapman to speak but a train accident delayed him in another town. Sunday began to preach from the Bible text of Mark 10:17.

"A rich young man came to Jesus," Billy said. "He had run to Jesus and kneeled down in front of him asking, 'How do I inherit eternal life?' Jesus told him to sell everything and follow him. Sadly he went away."

"A rich young man came to Jesus."

The crowd sat in silence waiting for the next word from Billy. "We never know what a man is worth until after he has been tested. No man is stronger than his weakest point. Jesus didn't ask anything unreasonable. God doesn't go half way but demands all. He has every right to demand our very best."

Besides improving Sunday's speaking skills and teaching him how to preach from the Bible, Chapman also encouraged Billy to improve his appearance and clothing. As another local newspaper wrote, "Sunday doesn't look like a preacher. He would more likely be taken as a speculator on the stock exchange or a prematurely old young business man. But when he launches into his sermon, you stop thinking about the man, and have to think about what he is saying."

More than dress and meetings, Chapman also taught Billy how to handle money. During his

"No man is stronger than his weakest point."

meetings, Chapman didn't call much attention to money. An offering was taken in the meeting but they never pressured the people to give money.

"I've learned to lean on the Holy Spirit," Chapman told his young assistant, "rather than on the things of this world." The evangelist took a modest salary for himself and his staff workers. Chapman's idea of fun was spending a few days or couple of weeks in a vacation home on Winona Lake, Indiana.

Because Chapman didn't have a lot of money, he purchased the vacation home in payments. Many years later in 1908, Chapman offered to sell the home to Billy and Nell Sunday. To the Sundays' surprise, Chapman said, "We've got to sell this place because we can't afford to keep the property. We still owe $1,500 on the mortgage." Billy and Nell loved this home on the lake and purchased it for

Chapman didn't call much attention to money.

enjoying vacations and family. The experience reinforced a lesson from Chapman—don't seek money while serving Christ.

Besides his speaking, evangelist Chapman wrote a short book entitled *Received Ye the Holy Ghost?* This book helped Billy focus his attention on the risen Christ instead of worldly treasures. Billy's attention turned to prayer and spending time alone with God. Many churches requested that Sunday and Nell speak at their conferences on prayer. Billy grew close in his friendship with Mr. Chapman.

One day between his meetings for Chapman, Sunday's daughter, Helen climbed onto his lap. Helen had just started school.

"Papa," she said, "let's go to bed and tell stories."

Billy shook his head from side to side. "I can't do it, Helen. I have to go away."

Helen stuck her hands on her hips. "Where are

Helen climbed onto his lap.

you going to, Papa?"

"Well," Billy said, "I've got to go to Urbana, Ohio, and then to Troy and, then to Evansville, and after that to Richmond and then to Indianapolis."

Helen wrinkled her brow and said, "Papa, you're the best friend I've got, and I don't want you to go away. Let's go to bed and tell stories."

"But I must go away, my dear, and if you will be a nice little girl and not cry, I will get you a present," Billy said as he tried to turn her attention somewhere else. Hesitantly, Helen agreed to receive a dress and a little ring. While on his trip, Sunday bought a silk dress with a blue stripe. When Helen saw it, she danced around in joy.

Another day, Helen came to her dad and said, "Papa, I don't want a dress. I just want you. You're the best friend I've got. Stay at home with me, Papa, and I won't ever want anything but you!"

"I don't want you to go away."

With sadness, Sunday realized his job took him away from his family. Billy saw how much his daughter cared about his days away from home. But then he reflected about the Christian life, "That's how we should be as Christians. The greatest desire of our hearts should be to live with Jesus— someone we've not seen but love."

Sunday realized his job took him away from his family.

"Nell, look at this telegram from Dr. Chapman."

7
Evangelist

"Nell, look at this telegram from Dr. Chapman," Billy called into the other room. "It's unbelievable." Only a few weeks earlier, Chapman and the Sundays had separated for their winter break during November and December.

Throughout his evangelistic ministry, Dr. Chapman was invited to lead different churches. In November, Dr. Chapman received the unexpected request to pastor his former church, Bethany Presbyterian Church in Philadelphia. As usual, this man of prayer turned to God for answers. Without consulting Billy Sunday or anyone else on his evangelistic team, Dr. Chapman decided to accept the job of pastor and leave his ministry.

Right in the middle of the Christmas holidays, Billy called Nell into the room to read the telegram from Dr. Chapman. The young couple felt stunned at the news. Suddenly Billy was out of work with a wife and two children to support. Should he return to baseball? No, he had been away from the sport for too many years. Should he return to the YMCA in Chicago? No, from his experience with Chapman, Billy knew his ministry was evangelism and revivals. The couple turned to the Heavenly Father for answers about their future.

"We're learning, Lord," Billy prayed, "that you don't free our lives from problems but you give us the strength to continue with our faith." Then Billy thought, "Faith is the beginning of something of which you can't see the end, but in which you believe." In a short time, Billy's faith would be

he couple turned to the Heavenly Father for answers.

honored.

The family continued with their Christmas holi-day celebration. Six days later, Billy received a second telegram. Sunday had never met the man who sent the telegram which read, "A Methodist preacher, a Baptist preacher and I have united. We're going to hold a revival in our town of Garner, Iowa. We've rented the Opera House already and we'd like to know whether you will come to lead us in our revival."

At the same time, Billy was excited and numb. The Sundays hugged and rolled with joy onto their living room carpet. Their prayers had been an-swered. "I don't know anyone in Garner, Iowa," Billy said, "but I'm going to tell them, 'yes.'"

Billy learned that Garner, Iowa was a rural farm community about forty miles south of the Minne-sota line. Before these ten days in Garner, Sunday

Their prayers had been answered.

had never held a meeting alone. In fact, Billy only had eight sermons and now he needed ten. When he arrived at the revival, there was no team with him and the choir only had twenty people. On the final day of the meeting, they took up an offering for Billy's expenses. They collected $68.

While Sunday held these meetings in Garner, the pastors in Sigourney, Iowa asked Billy to hold meetings in their city. No one knew that on January 9, 1896, Billy Sunday had begun a series of evangelistic preaching that would last the next forty years!

Billy and Nell were sitting on the front porch talking one evening about his ministry. "Some people think an evangelist has an easy life," Billy said. "You travel around, preach the same sermons, collect money from the offering and people come to Christ."

Nell agreed, "That's not half of it. You often set up the tent, rally the churches and handle many

"That's not half of it."

details concerning the event."

Billy continued, "I meet some interesting people, but getting there isn't easy. The train seats are upright and hard. When the weather is warm the dust and soot from the engine blows onto my clothes. And when it is cold, the windows are closed but the doors are drafty. The noise from the trains make sleep nearly impossible. So much for glamour," he said with a laugh.

"But my reason for going is something other than my physical comfort," Billy said. "There are people in the Kerosene Circuit who need Christ. They are carrying burdens which need to be laid down at the foot of the cross. Someone has to challenge them to make a decision and God has given me that honor."

"The Kerosene Circuit" is what Billy called the small towns where he preached. While the Sun-

"So much for glamour."

days lived in the big city of Chicago, these rural farm communities didn't have gas or electricity. Instead these people used kerosene lanterns to light their way in the evenings. During the first twelve years of his ministry, Billy preached in these remote places. Often he didn't know his schedule more than several weeks in advance. While Billy spoke in one town, another would invite him to come as soon as possible. These early meetings were held in local churches which only held one or two hundred people. Sometimes a town hall was available and several hundred to a thousand people could attend the services.

Gradually the young evangelist drew larger crowds. For his spring, summer and fall crusades, Billy would rent large canvas tents. While the tents could hold more people, they were not perfect. If the weather was warm, the tent flaps were lifted so

Billy would rent large canvas tents.

the air could circulate. In these days before microphones, sometimes Sunday had to strain to keep the crowd's attention from wandering. Other times the strong wind of the mid-west would blow down a tent pole or make the flaps pop. There were many physical challenges for Sunday, but he knew how to keep the crowd's attention.

When Sunday held a revival, it was for several weeks. Often he spoke every night for three weeks during these early days. Entire towns in the mid-west changed. In Emerson, Iowa, the newspaper reported, "Over a hundred were converted during the three weeks' meetings. Our little town has never witnessed such a transformation. A packed audience filled the opera house every night to hear Mr. Sunday. The evangelist's power in holding the close attention of his audience is wonderful."

As Sunday drew people to his preaching each

Often he spoke every night for three weeks.

night, the town of Emerson began to talk about the evangelist. Several farmers met at the local black-smith shop and began talking. "See here, Jones, there was never any preachin' done jes' like that baseball man does. I tell you, John, he's got more life in him than any two-year-old colt you ever saw. I would never of believed it if I hadn't a seen it. I didn't know anybody could be so much in earnest in his preaching."

John stood listening with intensity at his friend as he continued. "He's got a platform to stand on more'n as big as two wagon boxes, and he covers every inch of it in every sermon he preaches," the farmer waved his arms to show an example. "Why in the meeting last Sunday afternoon, he got so fired up that he tore off his coat and vest, jerked off his collar and then rolled up his sleeves as if he was a going to help thrash the devil." People didn't fall

John stood listening with intensity at his friend.

asleep when Billy Sunday spoke to the crowd. Every night people made decisions to change the direction of their lives and follow Christ.

After Emerson, Billy traveled by train to Malvern, Iowa for another three weeks of meetings. When Sunday stepped off the train, he could tell that some people were watching him closely. Rumors had spread through the town about the evangelist and his meetings. Some of the talk was upbeat about the meetings. Others downplayed Sunday's speaking ability and his work for the Lord.

People came early to the Baptist Church, which held over a thousand people. Soon the crowd overflowed into the aisles and outside. Through open windows people gathered to hear the evangelist. Sunday began to preach and held the attention of the crowd night after night. One of the local newspapers wrote, "His manner is magnetic, and his

Billy traveled by train to Malvern.

smile is so winsome that any heart goes toward him. Talk with Billy for five minutes and you will feel that he is an old friend." While in the town for the three weeks of meetings, Sunday put on his baseball uniform in the afternoons and played with the locals. The same newspaper article reported, "There is none of the puffed-up Pharisee about Sunday and that's why he is so well liked by those to whom he preaches."

The people filled the rows of seats for the final night of the meeting. A large choir led the singing. A series of songs began every meeting. Then Sunday preached for an hour or two to the people. No one moved when Sunday was shadow boxing with the devil on stage. "Men, today you are nursing a habit!" Billy raised his voice. "God pity you! You took it when it was an infant and today it is a giant, and is beating every streak of manhood out of you."

"God pity you!"

Then Sunday turned to his female audience, "Girls, you flirted with some Tom-Dick-and-Harry on the street; today your virtue is dragged up and down the highways. God pity you!"

In his preaching, Sunday mixed stories about people with stories from the Bible. The messages built to a climax. Billy finished the message saying, "There is a spot in Chicago, 100 E. Van Buren Street, where one Sunday night I walked in and got down at the altar and fought the battle with the devil and won. How I love to walk back and look at that spot where I fought and won the victory for God."

In the Malvern, Iowa meeting, 230 people committed their lives to Jesus Christ. Billy's fearless preaching and Bible–based sermons were changing people's lives.

One evening in a small town in Indiana, Sunday looked at the black sky. It was threatening to storm

"I fought the battle with the devil and won!"

that evening. He decided to sleep in the large revival tent. Through hard experience, Billy learned
that sometimes a thunderstorm completely wrecked
the tent. This evening the storm dumped rain on
Indiana and the lightening crashed. All night long
like a sailor on a ship during a storm, Billy tight-
ened the tent stakes and adjusted the ropes so the
tent wouldn't fall down.

If bad weather didn't threaten the meetings, Sunday slept in a hotel or with local pastors. In each
town, the local pastors or Christians fed Billy heap-
ing plates of fried chicken, potatoes and gravy. Billy
didn't gain weight because every night he worked
it off in his preaching and also in keeping his tent
from falling down.

After ten years of preaching revivals, Billy needed
some help and was finally able to afford it. In 1905,
he hired the "Cowboy Evangelist" named Fred

Sometimes a thunderstorm completely wrecked the tent.

Siebert. When the two men talked, Billy said, "Fred, your responsibilities will include doing some advance work, erecting the tents, then watching the facilities at night and some preaching." Billy felt relieved to find someone to help with these particular details of the crusades.

Despite the success of his revivals, Billy felt he needed to be ordained. Before his ordination at Jefferson Park Presbyterian Church in Chicago, Sunday appeared before a number of Bible college professors and other well-versed Christians in his church. For more than an hour, they asked questions to the former baseball player.

Professor Zenos of McCormick Theological Seminary asked Billy a question about St. Augustine. Sunday replied, "He didn't play for the National League. I didn't know him."

Then another one of the members of the board,

"I didn't know him."

Dr. Herrick Johnson, said, "Mr. Moderator, I move this needless examination stop. What difference does it make if he knows about Alexander, Savonarola and Cleopatra? God has used Billy to win more souls to Christ than all of us combined. He must have ordained Billy long before we ever thought of it. I move he be admitted to the Presbytery and we give him the right hand of fellowship and the authority of the Presbyterian Church." Dr. Johnson ended any further questions. The committee voted to ordain Sunday.

Before a packed crowd at Jefferson Park Presbyterian Church, Sunday was ordained in 1905. His old friend and associate in evangelistic work, Dr. J. Wilbur Chapman preached the sermon. Now Billy Sunday became "the Reverend Billy Sunday."

On September 20, 1906, the Billy Sunday team arrived in Salida, Colorado for a month of meet-

"I move he be admitted to the Presbytery."

ings. The sky was a clear blue and the days were warm with cool evenings. It looked perfect. After four weeks of beautiful weather, an unexpected heavy snow fell one evening. Early the next morning, the people in the town found five inches of heavy, wet snow. Some of the leaf-covered tree branches had broken from the snow. Sunday walked over to his revival tent. The weight of the snow had crushed the tent and destroyed the poles.

In his meetings, Billy didn't take a free will offering for each revival until the final night. Now it looked like he wouldn't receive money from the people for his work in this town. He worried about transportation for himself and the team to get home.

The Christians in the town shoveled snow out of the street and the final meeting was moved to a town hall. The small building only held half as many people as the tent but they gave generously.

The weight of the snow had crushed the tent.

Sunday didn't have to worry about traveling home. The destroyed tent marked a critical decision for Sunday. After they returned to Chicago, Billy told them, "No more tent meetings. From now on we'll erect a tabernacle or speak in buildings that are already in the town." If the town couldn't build a tabernacle, then Billy wouldn't come to the town. Once again, his ministry changed to a new direction.

"No more tent meetings."

"You'll need to build a wooden tabernacle."

8

From Tents to Tabernacles

Sunday couldn't forget the canvas tent covered with snow in Salida, Colorado. He made some major changes in his operation. Fred Siebert talked with local pastors about a possible Billy Sunday revival for their town.

"What is your largest meeting place in town?" Siebert asked.

"It only holds 500 people," one pastor responded.

"Well, the meetings will draw more people than that," Fred explained. "You'll need to build a wooden tabernacle at the expense of your local group of churches." These large buildings called tabernacles were used in the late 1890s and early

1900s. Evangelists like Wilbur Chapman and Dwight L. Moody had used these types of buildings for their meetings. In these wooden structures, meetings could be held without concern for the weather. As they were built, the community gained interest in attending the meetings.

Sunday began to only accept revivals where the town could build a tabernacle. After the meetings, these buildings were destroyed and the lumber sold.

As the size of the crowds increased, the number of decisions for Christ also grew. In Dixon, Illinois, the meetings received over a thousand new Christians and in Redwood Falls, Minnesota, over six hundred people accepted Christ. Billy saw increased church attendance after his revivals, and sometimes the bars lost so much business they had to close.

In 1909, Billy held his first revival in Spokane, Washington, which had over 100,000 people. It marked the largest city for his crusades. Now the

lly saw increased church attendance after his revivals.

Sunday team began to turn their attention to the masses. While he continued hold meetings in some small places, he spoke to larger groups of people.

While in the Pacific Northwest, Sunday began to talk about the sawdust trail. For years, loggers in a thick forest marked their trail with handfuls of sawdust. Then they followed the sawdust trail home. Newspaper reporters began to talk about the sawdust trail during Sunday's crusades. Thousands marched down the aisles when Billy called them home to Christ. Older men and women walked with young people, the prosperous banker walked with the construction worker. They came while the choir sang the verses of "Almost Persuaded." Many had tears streaming down their faces. As people walked forward during the invitation, Sunday leaped down from the platform to talk with the new Christians.

In 1916, five baseball players from the New York Yankees marched down the sawdust trail including

Many had tears streaming down their faces.

Frank "Home Run" Baker. Billy shook each player's hand and cheered as though they had just won the final game of the World Series. Home Run Baker told Billy, "No umpire ever received such a verbal slashing as you gave the devil. You make religion understandable—like eating, sleeping and playing baseball."

A large movement in the United States was trying to legally ban the sale of alcohol. It was called the Prohibition movement. While Billy Sunday wasn't a part of the political system, he certainly helped this movement through his sermons and talks against alcohol. For his services in Detroit, the churches combined to build the Gridley Field tabernacle which seated 16,000 people. At that time, it was the largest structure for a religious revival. One hundred and twenty Detroit churches suspended their Sunday morning services so their members could attend Sunday's revival services.

"You make religion understandable."

BILLY SUNDAY

A crowd of 3,000 greeted Billy when he stepped off the train. It was larger than the number of people who had turned out to see U.S. President Woodrow Wilson earlier that summer. Billy hadn't appeared in public in Detroit since his baseball years in the 1890s. As the people poured into the tabernacle for the opening service, Billy preached with excitement. He made the people laugh, shout, sing and cry. While praying, Sunday said, "Help Old Detroit. Throw your arms around her. Go into the barber shops, Lord, into the hotels, factories and saloons. Help the man on the street and the drunkard. The devil almost has him out. He's on the ropes and groggy, Lord. One more stiff uppercut will finish him. Help him, Lord, to square his shoulders and raise his dukes." Then the massive choir broke into the song, "Down in the Licensed Saloon," which was against alcohol.

During the several weeks of revival meetings in

"Help Old Detroit. Throw your arms around her."

Detroit, Sunday visited the estate of John S. Newberry and spoke to 300 members of the social elite. He also made a point of visiting factories and talking with the common worker.

At a noon–day talk with businessmen in Detroit, Sunday told them, "I'll chase the devil of alcohol from the moneybags of Griswold Street and shake it to death in the busy streets of commerce." Later that day, Billy visited the Ford plant and shook hands with the auto workers.

The final day of the Detroit crusade was on Sunday, November 5, 1916. Billy drew crowds of approximately 50,000 people. The next day, the Detroit News reported that according to the Bible, the Apostle Peter converted 3,000 on the day of Pentecost. On November 5, Billy Sunday watched 3,103 march forward down the sawdust trail and accept Christ. Just before the train pulled out of the Detroit station, Sunday told the crowd, "My mes-

Billy visited the Ford plant .

sage is all delivered. I leave you with God."

Over and over, doctors warned Billy to slow down. He and Nell rarely took vacations. Instead, as an evangelist, Sunday continued charging across the country and holding meetings at a rapid pace. In 1917, a doctor in Wichita warned Sunday, "If you don't slow down, you're headed for a nervous breakdown. Why don't you take a few weeks off?"

The stubborn evangelist shook his head and said, "I'll not quit preaching till I am compelled to do so. I'll preach till I break down. As long as I can get on the platform and talk, I'll give the devil a run for his money."

While on the road, Sunday found it nearly impossible to relax. On a train headed to Atlanta in 1917, a reporter asked Billy when he was going to stop the fast-paced life. Billy and Nell shook their heads. Then Nell said, "We've been talking about stopping for the last five years. I guess we'll be

"Why don't you take a few weeks off?"

talking about it for five years more, and then some."
There was so much work to be done, they said. How
could they stop?

In a rare moment at a small Indiana town called
Winona Lake, Sunday slowed down. Wearing an
old torn Panama hat, Billy puttered around the garden of the modest house. Sometimes Billy and Nell
would pack a picnic lunch, get into their car and
drive through the narrow winding roads and green
valleys.

Sunday was compiling some amazing statistics.
He personally spoke to more than 100 million people
during his 34 years of full evangelism. Over 200
wooden tabernacles were built for his revivals. Each
tabernacle could seat between 1,500 to 22,000
people.

In 1920, Billy called his team together. They
numbered 17 experts and five assistants. "I'm afraid
we've got to cut back our staff," he began. "Thank

In a rare moment Sunday slowed down.

you for your ministry to the team and to Christ." When he finished speaking, the team had narrowed to five experts. The Sunday revivals continued but in 1930, the team was officially dissolved.

As Billy grew older, he grew increasingly nervous and irritable on the platform for the revivals. Homer Rodeheaver was Sunday's music director for almost two decades. One day in 1927, Rodey wrote Nell Sunday about his some of his concerns about Billy.

"I'm writing to tell you about some problems with our meetings," Rodey began. "For several years, I've had some concerns about Billy. For the last several years, Billy has grown increasingly edgy before he preaches. Sometimes while Virginia Asher and I are singing a duet, he will stop us in the middle of the song and lay his Bible on the podium between us."

During some of these services, Billy would pace

"Billy has grown increasingly edgy."

the platform during the singing and special music. He had forgotten that music was built into the fabric of the service, and the songs had been carefully selected to prepare the people. Rodey felt that Billy had changed. Now the music was more of a bother to Sunday.

In his letter, Rodey also complained that Billy preached too long. "An hour and a half is too long and especially when Billy begins to speed up his message so the people can't understand what he is saying."

Finally Rodey suggested that Billy pushed too hard for himself and the staff. Often Billy and the staff worked seven days a week then didn't get two weeks off between meetings.

Nell received the letter and read it carefully. She managed many of the business aspects of the revivals. Despite these problems with the revivals, she told Rodey, "I can't pass this letter on to Billy.

Billy pushed too hard for himself and the staff.

It will only bother him and bring more tension into his life." A few months later, Rodey quietly left the Sunday organization, remaining good friends with Billy and Nell.

In the autumn of 1935, Billy and Nell were packing for a trip to Chicago from their home in Winona Lake, Indiana. Just before they closed their suitcases, Rodey knocked on their back door. Along with the younger men, Rodey called Sunday "Boss."

"Boss, I've been preaching at the First Methodist Church in Mishawaka, Indiana, but something's come up," Rodey explained. "I've got to go to Washington, D.C. Will you be strong enough to preach for me?"

Billy said, "Yes, Rodey, I'm feeling fine. I'd like to go."

Instantly Nell protested, "Billy, the doctor said that you weren't to take any more meetings."

The evangelist pounded his table and growled,

Instantly Nell protested.

"I guess I know how I feel."

With some hesitation, Nell said, "All right. If that's the way you want it, we'll go."

The couple drove over to Mishawaka which was about fifty miles from their home. That Sunday afternoon, it rained hard so the crowd was small. For his Bible text, Billy used the question from the Philippian jailer. The jailer asked, "What must I do to be saved?" When Sunday gave the invitation, forty-four people walked forward to accept Christ. Billy and Nell were thrilled!

That night marked the last message for Billy Sunday and the last number of people who came forward on the sawdust trail. The next week the couple drove to Chicago. While helping Nell's brother Will Thompson in the yard, suddenly Billy said, "I'm feeling tired and cold, Nell. I'd best lay down and get some rest."

"I'd best lay down and get some rest."

Later Nell brought Billy a bowl of cold cereal and cream. They ate the cereal together out of one bowl and talked over a cup of tea. Nell walked downstairs to turn off the oven. In the kitchen she heard a shout, "Nell! Oh, come quick! I've got an awful pain!" Across his chest and along both arms, Billy hurt. After they called a doctor, he came to the house and gave Billy an ice pack for his chest. Finally Billy rested comfortably.

Nell sat beside his bed and wrote some letters. While she was writing, suddenly she heard Billy's voice, "I'm getting dizzy, Ma!" He sighed and slipped into heaven.

Sunday's loud voice was silent. During his lifetime, he preached to over 100 million people and in thirty-nine years more than a million people made a public commitment to Jesus Christ.